IMPERFECT PRAYERS

RICHARD CARR

Richard Carr's ten-line *Imperfect Prayers* are not religious poems. They are late-night cries for mercy, meditations on the spiritual truths of grocery shopping and dental procedures, and maddened love letters to the creator of constellations and children without limbs. As Jacob wrestled with the angel, this poet struggles toward intimacy with a mysterious, sometimes infuriating God, confessing that "[he] will never comprehend him." Comprehension—perhaps not. But with the creator "cupping both his hands over [the poet's] fist and jittery pen," Carr searches for God—and, I believe, finds him—in a frozen lake, a buzzing cicada, a flickering computer screen: "everywhere his un-bearable odor and love."

—TANIA RUNYAN, AUTHOR OF *SIMPLE WEIGHT* AND
A THOUSAND VESSELS

Imperfect Prayers

RICHARD CARR

STEEL TOE BOOKS

Bowling Green, Kentucky

ISBN 978-0-9824169-6-9

STEEL TOE BOOKS
Western Kentucky University
Department of English
1906 College Heights Blvd. #11086
Bowling Green, KY 42101-1086
steeltoebooks.com

COVER PHOTOGRAPH
"Jacob Wrestling with the Angel" by Alexander Louis Leloir, 1865

COVER AND BOOK DESIGN
Molly McCaffrey

STEEL TOE BOOKS is affiliated with Western Kentucky University.

CONTENTS

1. God tells me to make poems about his creation

2. I tell God it will be difficult to obey him

3. God assures me that imperfect prayers are heard

4. I object to the secrecy

5. God sympathizes

6. I worry about the death of contradiction

7. God gently reminds me of his duality

8. I wish God were more specific

9. God replies with silence

10. I refuse to worship God

11. God appreciates my concern

12. I despise my poverty

13. God opens doors for me

14. I accept God's help dishonestly

15. God understands my reluctance to face him

16. I prefer a less intimate relationship

17. God retreats to the suburbs of consciousness

18. I look for comrades in the light of the city

19. God finds me in moments of crisis

20. I want independence

21. God pays dearly for my education

22. I flaunt orphan credentials

23. God shakes his head

24. I call out to God when I am in pain

25. God knocks out the lights in my neighborhood

26. I reduce God to his constituent parts

27. God scrubs the sky clean

28. I wash my hair morosely

29. God exceeds the dimensions of the world

30. I thank God for all these words

31. God promises me things will get better

32. I prowl like a sleepwalker

33. God guarantees the sunset

34. I waste God's time

35. God skips work some days

36. I smother my ambition in the garage

37. God indulges my dramatics

38. I pry open God's pocket knife while he's not looking

39. God mocks my pain

40. I copy down everything God says

41. God smooths my hair in the morning

42. I send messages to God in code

43. God sings to me

44. I compose human music

45. God prohibits self-absorbed celibacy

46. I blink wildly

47. God freezes the lake in the winter

48. I answer God's prayers

49. God charts his course upward

50. I fondle an ice cream cone

51. God makes truths that wear out

52. I undermine the hopes of my neighbors

53. God trims lawns and paints houses

54. I fritter away God's trust

55. God laughs

56. I defy God with my nakedness

57. God outsmarts the schoolboy

58. I disappoint God

59. God returns to the dust from which he came

60. I detest the condos across the lake

61. God compels my obedience

62. I accelerate the violence of the cosmos

63. God loves my gall

64. I anticipate the aches and pains of my old age

65. God advertises an afterlife in his presence

66. I fear death

67. God denies my existence

68. I follow the dragonfly

69. God kisses me on the lips

70. I moonlight denying home loans

71. God issues frightening ultimatums

72. I peruse the fine print on my grocery coupons

73. God extorts my silence

74. I feel free with God

75. God touches my nose

76. I sit at the rain-blurred window

77. God counts the days

78. I burn one day at a time

79. God sets half the city ablaze in time of war

80. I pray loud

81. God vacations alone

82. I miss my family

83. God reverses my fortune

84. I emerge in the spring naked and cold

85. God wrestles with his demons

86. I blame God for my failures

87. God climbs the stairs with me

88. I grovel under flowering crabapples

89. God regards me with hooded eyes

90. I write God a jingle

91. God flips through a magazine

92. I go to God with my cleverest ideas

93. God feeds my fish while I am away

94. I excuse myself from the table

95. God prepares a special death for me

96. I live only for God

97. God acts a little crazy in my dreams

98. I walk away from my job at the uptown bistro

99. God torments my free moments

100. I brush my teeth correctly

101. God passes through the garden in the winter

1.

God tells me to make poems about his creation,
green lakes with acres of blue sky,
the sudden boiling of thunderheads,

also bricks, the two-story storefront,
the gift shop with its candles and little boxes of stationery,
the bistro next door, monochromatic, unfriendly in daylight,

and the piles of uncollected garbage in the alley,
twenty-seven bags attracting only three flies so far
who buzz loops in the air in their joy,

and I will fly loops in the sky.

2.

I tell God it will be difficult to obey him
because I don't believe in flying men
except in a man-made airplane

and in my dreams of silver wings,
for even with all his famous might,
he could not lift me an inch above the bed

but in fact does all he can to throw down the airplane,
fill it with spiraling, dizzy terror
and crush the screaming thing against the earth,

which jolts me in my sleep.

3.

God assures me that imperfect prayers are heard,
that the bad prayers of the dying
help a little,

that breast tumors and switchback roads
can be survived
with concentration and adequate training,

and as for the mystery of suffering,
the protruding bone of it,
teens in car wrecks, fleas, nothing on TV tonight,

death dissolves it quickly, like a sugar cube in black coffee.

4.

I object to the secrecy,
knowing coffee contains caffeine,
then not knowing,

visualizing the water molecule as three ping-pong balls,
only smaller, and more colorful, like doughnut sprinkles,
agitated but clinging together in the boil

inexplicably, bound in theory
like a family ready to explode, the daughter volatile,
and no amount of coffee can stop it

or expose the agent of their grief.

5.

God sympathizes,
our headaches his headache,
our endless war inextricably linked to his,

our prisons, interrogation rooms, lethal injections
hard to quit,
like the habit of punching some bastard's face in the bar

or talking down to a friend
as though to a lesser being, in a lower order of drunken angels,
like backhanding your girlfriend across the jaw that night

knowing precisely the origin of evil.

6.

I worry about the death of contradiction,
the pain pills, the sterile hospital setting,
desperate to go peacefully,

having it both ways, doctor and priest both
calling double vision vision,
everyone in maddening agreement,

and no one willing to admit I'm not a man anymore
but a mechanism of nature, a solemn shrieking ape
thrown out of the clinic,

chased out of the temple.

7.

God gently reminds me of his duality,
a flash of lightning flooding the treetops
blotting out eyesight,

the crow on my windowsill unmoved,
curious about some shiny object in my room,
the candy dish,

or his own reflection, an exact copy,
except one shimmers with life,
then shivers with thunder, an afterthought,

snakes of rain hissing in the leaves.

8.

I wish God were more specific,
more like a classical statue, naked and angry
but solid, morally handsome,

or a comic book hero,
always around when you need him,
colorful, entertaining,

a little lonely, the friend of children,
creator of toys, candy eggs, leukemia,
the nightlight,

a fat mother-deity harvesting rice.

9.

God replies with silence
which he expects me to fill with prayer
somehow at the bus stop, noisiest corner on the street,

better during my nap, quietest hour of the afternoon,
four p.m., when everyone at work wishes they were elsewhere
and I snore perfectly

until the evening news,
a glass of wine, sunset on the curtains,
and before bed comb my hair thoughtfully

looking in the mirror for that prayer I forgot.

10.

I refuse to worship God,
or love him,
or make eye contact,

the thought of him
a cat melting into the rain
among tomato plants,

memory a toothache
waking me abruptly in the morning,
still raining hard in the garden,

cat out there somewhere.

11.

God appreciates my concern,
shrugging it off with indifferent thanks,
for he lives in ample luxury without me,

and in his city of glass towers and palm-lined avenues
where everyone dresses like playing-card kings and queens,
he writes the big checks,

owns mountains, the blue lake, the white cloud,
and silver constellations, endless rangelands of light
in which I am only a few atoms,

carefully constructed, but forgettable.

12.

I despise my poverty,
toaster oven, raisin bagel, Don Giovanni,
a view of trees, big mortgage,

grumble about my wealth,
a boxelder bug crawling on a slat of the blinds,
lonely,

mope to the store for cream cheese and tea,
bump against the electric door
like a bird, amazed

when the glass moves aside.

13.

God opens doors for me
not that I can't fend for myself
with the crutches he gave me

and ply my trade quite independently
scraping gum from under chair seats for its remnant of flavor
and sanding down bathroom graffiti for the spicy dust

though it's nice when he puts his hand on my back
and walks with me through the service tunnel
to the utility room with its bare bulb and desk

and cups both his hands over my fist and jittery pen.

14.

I accept God's help dishonestly,
gazing upward in thanks,
looking right through him and out the window,

seeking inspiration in dull nature,
autumn wind, collapsed pumpkin,
frosty exhaust vapors swirling behind a passing car,

but his breath on my neck tingles, like wet ice, and I shy away,
naming him over and over
like the geese overhead honking his name

until it fades in the distance.

15.

God understands my reluctance to face him
whose look bends knees, burdens shoulders,
forces tears to burst from both eyes at once,

leaving only the rug to look at, and it dazzles,
or the dirt, the pavement, with their deep holes,
or shoes, worthless feet,

and toenails, created in his likeness,
and fungus, in his likeness,
blood, pus, likeness,

and everywhere his unbearable odor and love.

16.

I prefer a less intimate relationship,
like encountering a fox in the rail yard
who knows something about hauling coal

and pauses on the tracks to show me his superiority,
trots under an open boxcar, looks back,
testing his bravery,

for we are both trespassers,
one heavy and harmless, like a pallet of lumber,
the other a frail ember, nourished by the breeze,

one turning toward sunset, one following at a distance.

17.

God retreats to the suburbs of consciousness,
fades from relevance overnight, and is forgotten,
like roller skates and board games in a jumbled closet,

almost forgotten, like a wedding ring in a safe-deposit box,
love letters in a dresser drawer,
phone numbers on napkins,

not quite forgotten,
yet left untouched, like cave paintings in charcoal and ocher,
voluptuous horses, aurochs, deer, forever leaping,

always there, but covered in darkness.

18.

I look for comrades in the light of the city,
the amber glow of winter smog
which from a distance is a vast meteorological phenomenon

though up close it's only streetlights and holiday decorations,
sluggish evening traffic,
flashing TV screens in living room windows,

track lighting in the coffee shop,
the buzzing blue aura of the gas station,
a yellow bulb in the front porch,

my bedside lamp, an open book.

19.

God finds me in moments of crisis,
hitting the airbag in a hard kiss,
my bear skin of whisky and beer gone maggoty,

and I drop to my knees on the pavement,
blood trickling on my scalp like rivulets of rain,
streetlight, asphalt, headache,

but still no prayer, while God watches,
a ghost or reflection in the night-dark deli window,
sirens, though I don't need help,

don't want help.

20.

I want independence,
secure borders, international waters,
free sailing,

insolent solitude,
purple haze, malaise, cold war,
peace, with or without honor,

want black limousine, ice cream,
cuddly trophy,
free agency at any price,

want playtime, home, latchkey and alone.

21.

God pays dearly for my education,
an irksome expense, like out-of-state tuition,
while I grow long hair and insult him from a distance

in sophomore essays and lazy thinking on Saturday afternoons
about a better world,
clean and green and so much better

than the mess he's made,
he and his followers, my tutors and straightlaced classmates,
whom I treat like fools,

tossing them off and waving my hair.

22.

I flaunt orphan credentials,
as though I sprung like a spindly pine
from fire-charred soil,

keeping secret my false identity behind a whirling cape,
black mask, heavy gloves,
fog of noble purpose,

a storybook genius inventing lightbulbs, energy, mass,
the speed of light, and light itself,
the bomb,

every perfection and quirky flaw all mine.

23.

God shakes his head,
flashing between amusement and fury
like sunlight off a lake,

like a gossamer lifted on the breeze,
a bright green worm wriggling on the end,
shakes his mighty head sadly,

shakes decisively,
a fish leaping from the water to catch the worm,
splash back through the scattered surface

and swim stiffly away.

23

24.

I call out to God when I am in pain
without expecting results
and press my elbow into my ribs until the pain passes

not expecting to die today
still willing
still certain my limp hand will revive

asleep in throbbing stasis
arm folded against chest like the blackened limb of a ditch corpse
which to move even an inch

invites the screams of the dead.

25.

God knocks out the lights in my neighborhood,
and I go out walking, calm in the same calm darkness
through which the original angels fell,

candles in the corner bistro flickering on the diners' faces
as they cut their meat with flickering knives,
stab russet potatoes,

lively and smiling,
realizing new plans for the new night,
more wine,

and light, in secret desiring more light.

26.

I reduce God to his constituent parts,
the universe and not the universe,
and yet cannot put my finger on him

let alone embrace
or love what I cannot find,
poor God standing right behind me

while I fish in my pocket for pennies
to make exact change at the coffee counter,
come up short, unfold a crumpled bill

and drop the worthless surplus in the tip jar.

27.

God scrubs the sky clean,
never quite white,
but fresh and wet and glistening,

and I put blue into it,
blue of happiness, blue of freedom, blue of loneliness,
watercolor blue

that blackens as night burns the paper firmament
and flecks it with bright ashes
which in turn wash away in the morning

when God gets on his knees to work.

28.

I wash my hair morosely,
hands and hair mutually incomprehensible,
but they are in love

and exchange gifts,
a bracelet made of braided candy wrappers,
drugstore sunglasses,

while in the privacy of a beach umbrella
they do not touch,
each too perfect for the other,

until the sad evening and the wordless union.

29.

God exceeds the dimensions of the world,
like an overfull dumpster in the summer
spilling bags and moldy boxes into a river of trash,

the Mississippi rising, spreading through the city,
coming in through the front door and the back door
to the height of the couch-back, pillows floating,

like the grief of those who lose their children in the looting
and know nothing is safe,
nothing kept out by plywood nailed over windows,

nothing held in.

30.

I thank God for all these words
but live in fear that he will take away my shoes
or eyesight

drain my car battery in an empty parking lot after dark
lampposts towering in a blizzard
memory depleted of landmarks and laws

isolate me in a hospital wing
with crippled shoulders
and a mirror

a piece of paper and a dried-out pen.

31.

God promises me things will get better,
that maimed children will grow new limbs,
excel in sports, and praise him,

that the last bees will survive
somehow
in a world without nectar, paradise without flowers,

that I will prosper
in a growth economy of souls expanding infinitely,
absurdly hopeful

for one lying between icy cold sheets.

32.

I prowl like a sleepwalker,
two cooling towers at the nuclear plant
steaming drowsily in the moonlight,

trucks passing on the highway, time passing in gusts,
though I do not spin in the wind
or drink the wash of exhaust,

a flame of idea cupped in my hand,
a lively orange-green flicker
emitting oily threads of smoke,

my own beautiful pollution of the industrial night.

33.

God guarantees the sunset,
his incandescence cutting through trees on the hilltop,
the dairy farm below already gathered for sleep,

his brilliance chrome-plating the endless turnpike,
his sheen on the pavement
the metallic pang of an old wound,

his reflection on a lake a chasm of light
bubbling over with stars,
the little fisherman in his boat dissolving in blindness,

in light that is agony to the witness.

34.

I waste God's time
not that he's in any hurry
being a patient scientist

the universe confined to its test tube
slowly turning green
while he observes his creation

time
a garden buried under snow
ripples in window glass

I in my robe.

35.

God skips work some days,
stays home in bed staring at the ceiling,
unresolved, the clock ticking forward and backward,

and I throw down my tools,
another day wasted,
and walk restlessly in the hall

thinking about lunch,
a can of tomato soup, white-bread sandwiches,
which cannot be made

without his mighty will.

36.

I smother my ambition in the garage,
sweeping sawdust into the oil stain,
stapling black tarp over the window,

unscrewing the bare bulb,
car hood still hot,
air thick, toxic,

God crowding me with his darkness,
my vision dotted with spangles of light,
pale-eyed devils in the rafters

at home in my solitude.

37.

God indulges my dramatics
as a form of worship,
a theatrical homage to his mystery,

but prefers despair and paralysis,
quiet meditation upon his greatness
and the limits of his beneficence,

encouraging pure existential terror
as a fitting substitute for love,
clear-eyed, without expectations,

true love.

38.

I pry open God's pocket knife while he's not looking
and touch the blade,
my finger wrapped in a sticky bandage

from last time,
this time no different,
the blood and sting as sudden as ever

and always a little surprising,
as though the knife might not cut if I know it's sharp
and act quick,

so poorly do I understand his forgiveness.

39.

God mocks my pain,
filling novels, movies, street corners, bedrooms with it,
splattering it in a crimson bus, in the chaotic hospital, on cable news,

tear-gassing the crowd outside the checkpoint,
back-stabbing, wrist-slitting,
teacher,

crossing the blue sky with the full rainbow of his violence,
firing rockets into the ground
where old men play cards

and boys call for death.

40.

I copy down everything God says,
not his mouthpiece,
or apostle,

but more like a student
puzzling over the homework assignment,
wishing I had asked more questions

too late,
dutiful nonetheless, teeth brushed before bed,
and sad, so bored all day

I will never comprehend him.

41.

God smooths my hair in the morning,
and I wake comforted,
dreamless,

no more the overturned vehicle at the underpass,
woman trapped inside, familiar,
scolding,

no more the cold morgue, concrete walls and blackened window,
nor the folded letter, sealed with its *xoxo*,
little tongue kisses,

caresses.

42.

I send messages to God in code,
technologically, posting my picture online
with obscured identity but true feelings,

biologically, arranging brain cells
in the shape of a difficult poem
which I expect him to parse,

philosophically, like Socrates in lively dialogue
with his dreary patsies and winking cronies,
a playful pretext for serious subtext,

symbolically, a wind-up monkey making urgent music.

43.

God sings to me
in the small voice of a fly
trapped in the medicine cabinet,

or in the big chorus of the city,
grinding garbage truck in the alley,
a thousand honking cabs, a shout in the street,

siren, jet, jackhammer a screaming trio,
or two dying crickets under the rug
chirping their liebestod,

the long-awaited resolution.

44.

I compose human music,
humming a song without words
in my dark bedroom,

knocking out deranged guitar chords,
fingers of stone
clamped crookedly on the frets,

then giving in to whistling in the shower,
ditties, not hymns,
but in tune and echoing

and equally disobedient.

45.

God prohibits self-absorbed celibacy,
demands family happiness,
children, school play, car pool,

as though prolonged solitude wasted his energy,
like a star burning in the sky all day
invisibly,

guiding no one,
delighting no eye,
exciting not the love-making couple

but the jobless poet walking in degenerate thought.

46.

I blink wildly
trying to correct my thinking
while God lights matches under unsuspecting neurons

spits rain in my eye
trips my tongue down the front steps
flips my feet in the air

and then I blink heavily
tying painful splints to my broken thoughts
while God stands silently over me

waiting impatiently for my next move.

47.

God freezes the lake in the winter
and so expresses his pain,
lonely, white,

grinding darkly beneath the surface,
while I walk the path along the smooth shore,
shielding my eyes from his immensity and stillness

even as my body turns toward him,
the comfort I offer
spent far out on the ice, a swirl of snowflakes lifted

and blown away.

48.

I answer God's prayers
if they are reasonable,
wash and dress in the morning

in his likeness,
two scarves wrapped around my neck,
black gloves in all seasons,

today a black shoulder bag, black boots,
black eyes,
as I browse the gift shop

for a trinket or charm to appease him.

49.

God charts his course upward,
contrary to our horizontal explorations,
our tedious sailing toward ever-retreating horizons,

and even in spacecraft
the universe unfurls infinitely,
our minds flattened as they stretch across the void,

cosmos after cosmos, island after island, certain
the gold and spices of enlightenment lie mounded on a far shore,
or uncertain, but unable to resist

looking out over the prow.

50.

I fondle an ice cream cone
like an intractable proposition
licking it with difficulty

applying a fool's logic
to the fast-melting problem
the lost drips

the sticky situation
developing too quickly
for the calculus of delectation

and the slow, love-making mouth.

51.

God makes truths that wear out,
like a pair of jeans,
comfortable, frayed, limited,

like the obsolete computer
unable to view pictures of grandkids,
though they are here somewhere,

or an old car in hard times
I won't let die
out of necessity and love

and daring ignorance of all else.

52.

I undermine the hopes of my neighbors
by parking with one wheel on the curb
and fumbling with keys at the front door angrily,

trees all down the street disturbed
by my strong gusts,
windows broken at the school,

and rain, swirling around everything,
drags down spirits from the heavens,
dashes them against the ground

among wet leaves too cold to rake.

53.

God trims lawns and paints houses,
yardboy of the dull devout
who with their nonchalance retain him,

certifying their achievements against pride,
guaranteeing their gardens against evil,
the apple tree undesirable and perfect,

while in the bedroom monkeys cling to the mirror
and the lights burn without meaning to,
warm water splashing in the tub,

cold water in my cup before bed.

54.

I fritter away God's trust,
the bank defunct, the polished vault of divine knowledge
cleaned out,

and so at last I pray,
derelict and prickly and wind-crossed,
and I want a better haircut, new shoes, french fries,

get hands wrapped like mummies,
stomach stuffed with grass, throat of clay,
the dry mouth open, like a bird's nest,

and of course no voice but the weedy scratching of the wind.

55.

God laughs,
a cicada buzzing viciously on a hot afternoon,
one loner, hidden in the leaves,

then one in every tree,
the stridulations piercing, impossible to ignore
as the heart races in perverse fear,

until nightfall
when the robin chirps furtively,
one alone, then one thousand tittering sociably

and no insect keen to be known.

56.

I defy God with my nakedness,
my feminine hat and vulnerable penis
not too delicate for warfare,

and again with my big hands and hammered feet,
my gaze lifted up carelessly
to permit full view of my divine musculature,

but at last with my own face,
schoolboy brave on the sandlot of battle,
biting my lip in concentration

as I aim a stone at his wild eye.

57.

God outsmarts the schoolboy
who prefers television and Oreos
to homework spread out on the kitchen table,

likes a big warm bed better than baseball and kites,
staring out the window at ugly starlings
better than cleaning his room,

wants a book about wizards,
and books about frontiersmen, riflemen,
astronauts, because they are free,

and Spartans sacking proud Athens brutally.

58.

I disappoint God,
completing my errand too literally
by coming home with milk, bread, lettuce, olive loaf

and summer-day hopes
for an afternoon free of needy mail
and flip calls

or any thoughts outside the white fence of eyesight,
green lawn,
happy with myself, weight, hair,

freckles.

59.

God returns to the dust from which he came
to nurture purple turtleheads and pink phlox
and give life to bees,

give intelligence to the wind,
exuberance and enterprise to the sun,
momentary hope to the garden visitor, hands in pockets,

who came to the park to despise God,
where no flower may be picked, nothing touched,
a snapshot permitted, but poor,

every green stem and yellow petal luminous with inscrutable purpose.

60.

I detest the condos across the lake,
fire-white walls, false red tiles,
Mediterranean balconies hovering above the hot beach,

the combed sand hissing and oily,
sunbathers watching television,
water off-limits,

reflected aircraft banking into a distant runway approach,
traffic on the shoreline drive always fast,
bicyclists, joggers, skaters on parade,

God pinning my arms behind my back.

61.

God compels my obedience
which is no obedience at all
but a low-paying job,

a hair in my egg salad sandwich
which I eat anyway
without question,

a blindness in the corner of one eye,
a dandelion in the other,
the tops of clouds rushing between them,

tray upright, seatbelt fastened.

62.

I accelerate the violence of the cosmos,
a lethargic driver, one thumb on the wheel,
speeding toward an abutment and an abrupt end,

whereas at the grocery I slow the line,
fumbling to make a neat pyramid
of ten items or less,

the edifice of thought meant to last forever,
not millennia, not mere moments,
but the bag boy only smiles, not helping,

and I drive out of the parking lot as it crumbles into the void.

63.

God loves my gall,
a chunk of bitter chocolate in the kitchen cupboard
unchanged by time,

embraces my resentment,
a pot of rice left to harden on the stove top
like a starched brain,

kisses away the blood of my dirty little wounds,
the paring knife that nicked my fingertip
lying weeks in the stainless sink unwashed

somehow precious to him.

64.

I anticipate the aches and pains of my old age
cracks in the driveway
dead limb on the maple tree

paint peeling on the garage door
broken shingles
cutworms aphids ladybirds mealybugs

memory loss
poor eyesight in the evening
neuralgic burning under my right cheekbone

shortness of breath when I walk in the back yard looking for God.

65.

God advertises an afterlife in his presence,
that Disneyland of eternal happiness
a bait-and-switch scam,

better to seek terrestrial bliss,
for there is no field in Elysium
where my father hunts pheasants,

no beer hall in Valhalla
where he waits at the end of a long bar
to hear my story,

Heaven rather a jumbled airport clogged with holiday travelers.

66.

I fear death,
fear God won't be there, in my bed
that day,

busy elsewhere
making phone calls
from the back of a cab,

fear I will pass away unnoticed
like an old dog curled up in the woods
becoming tufts of fur, deflated body,

snarling lips in a drift of leaves.

67.

God denies my existence,
which makes for a lonely breakfast
and hardly any daylight,

awkward when he walks into the room,
pours a glass of orange juice, flicks me a glance,
and goes out to the driveway,

floods the world with morning light,
lifts the arms of the trees,
and leaves me

alone with my sugar toast and no plans for the day.

68.

I follow the dragonfly,
circling the pond dizzy with hunger
and the gulping intensity of two months to live,

and I want to live,
each new thought
a new pleasing embrace of myself,

and the sparrow wants to live,
the sparrow's leviathan hunger
and swifter flight

an end to my ecstasy.

69.

God kisses me on the lips,
and his breath smells like a chicken coop in summer,
dismal, indelible,

industrial, ten thousand birds confined together,
dozens dead,
feather dust frilling the air,

no smoking,
hot,
a job I can't quit,

a boss who loves me.

70.

I moonlight denying home loans,
slitting envelopes, stamping applications,
happy to work methodically

though touched by the poverty of my countrymen,
their licking of stamps
and pressing hard with the pen,

their aspirations canny and ambitious, but half-starved,
like a gull hovering in a sea wind, ethereal,
until it sees a fish and plummets,

miss.

71.

God issues frightening ultimatums,
believe or die, love or die, live or die,
like a terrorist desperate to be heard,

and I do believe,
lake ice breaking up in a spring gale
dancing with his energy,

and I do love,
the tang of bacon and buttery eggs inside the diner
satisfying my special need,

but I will die, because that is how he makes himself known.

72.

I peruse the fine print on my grocery coupons,
the language of redemption and expiration
neat and legal

and mortally explicit,
one's value in life
nullified by the specificity of death,

day-old bread of little interest,
blackened bananas on sale,
red meat gone gray, iridescent, sticky,

the coupon brightly printed, the glossy tomato compelling.

73.

God extorts my silence
floods my mouth with non sequiturs
snaps my pencil in two for emphasis

for kicks
kicks me when I bend down
molests my sleep

pushes a thermometer up my ass
x-rays my lungs nine times in nine weeks
and gives me no prognosis

but what his false tears betray.

74.

I feel free with God,
all my feelings negated,
my ugliness loved,

skeleton cheeks and oblong eyes,
my toothy face untouchable
but dear to him,

fond in his sinister heart
of deformity, mutation, taboo,
and all the forces of creation

that make me a happy man.

75.

God touches my nose
but does not cure it of blackheads
rubs my neck but leaves it aching

heals my eye
split open looking at the sun
but gives it no vision

makes my shriveled tongue whole
unkinks my crippled hand
sews a button on my shirt

while I sit at the window in winter silence.

76.

I sit at the rain-blurred window,
incompetent,
pangs like hunger bothering me inside,

however pure the sound of falling water,
however comforting the slow pace of twilight
or the stillness made possible

in the process of dying,
cell by cell,
as the lights come on across the street

and I stop counting the days.

77.

God counts the days,
measures time maniacally,
tapping his watch, smiling brilliantly,

winds consciousness in a tangled skein,
too impatient with his knitting
to finish a thought,

engineers new pyramids
on every planet
for suns to circle, according to ancient law,

until they are all burned out.

78.

I burn one day at a time
each a virgin forest
each a saint

secrets in the house
a cigarette smoldering in the sofa
crossed wires sparking in the wall space

a feeling like grief in my throat
choking on water
smoke

flicking my Zippo compulsively.

79.

God sets half the city ablaze in time of war,
saves half,
agitating journalists but no one else,

starves all the children on whole continents
but not the soldiers,
horrifying humanitarians and no one else,

sickens rich and poor, sickens cattle and poultry,
sickens frogs,
alarming scientists, no one else,

because we pray to him, Death, who hears no prayer.

80.

I pray loud
out on the lawn sidestepping sprinklers
showing my neighbors what's what

and in the parking ramp downtown
where broken echoes cannot be healed
but harmonize with honking cars

and at the office before morning break
like a fire alarm piercing all cubicles
with my message

that God hears but fails to understand.

81.

God vacations alone
on a beach where no consciousness can reach him,
no word disturb a grain of sand,

towel spread out, big umbrella tilted
for shade,
and no one to be seen,

a cold, green drink sweating
on a book,
reading glasses, a key ring with one key,

the sound of waves working contentedly.

82.

I miss my family,
my dead friend, not dead yet,
my old cat,

the house, its gables and steep roof,
the flat lawn,
an old maple shedding bark,

the kitchen window where squirrels peered in,
a quiet lunch with company
like a sacrament,

no one speaking or planning to leave.

83.

God reverses my fortune so often
I am finally lulled
by the pointless dialectic,

and when he tempts me with friends and prostitutes,
as though mere frankness
would draw me out,

I withdraw further,
like a frog creeping into the mud for the winter,
not yet to die, but to a grave, at least,

of my own choosing.

84.

I emerge in the spring naked and cold
out of bed with a headache
swerving into the bathroom for a pill

and in the mirror a prairie crocus
purplish face with wispy gray whiskers
shivering

the last winter wind blowing through the warm house
scarves flapping on all the coat hooks
a pair of crumpled boots

the still-frozen sun rising pane by pane in the window.

85.

God wrestles with his demons
somewhere behind the curtain of stars,
unseen and unknowable,

and in his lonely apartment,
unpaid bills scattered on the coffee table,
he flicks the lights on and off,

while on Earth matter struggles with energy
and the welfare checks, pension checks, disability checks
fly in jets to their destinations

too late to save him.

86.

I blame God for my failures,
as though he stabbed my eyes out
and fed me soup of tepid discontent,

as though he authored my worst moments,
licking my lips in the long soliloquy against him,
plotting my complex demise,

as though he pushed me into the street
where I walk slowly through red lights and honking cars,
drunk on bile and vapid wine,

as though he made the rags I wear, the stairs I climb.

87.

God climbs the stairs with me
to the rooftop to make a point
about the altitude of his office

and in the dry air I feel his hand in mine
and it hurts
to see all the rooftops of the world

all the images of God and me
the wind lifting our hair in halos
in bewildering repetition

across a wild unaccountable country.

88.

I grovel under flowering crabapples,
chilled in spring drizzle,
and taste the fleshy musk of wet earth,

the weight of dark pink and sky white blossoms
pushing me to the ground,
subservient,

broken down to my knees by their bruising perfume,
primitive language of the multitude
that cuts X's in my guts

while I force my gaze upward.

89.

God regards me with hooded eyes,
the stoplight turning yellow
staring at me as I pass through,

the elevator that remains open behind me
as I walk down the hallway humming,
closing finally when I look back,

or my computer screen which flashes and goes blank
then pops on again, flickering angrily,
so that the next key I touch

had better be good.

90.

I write God a jingle
la la
and touch the pencil tip to my tongue

write him a novel
the end
and lick the envelope

write him a tablet of laws
thou mayst
and blow away the chips of stone

but still he wants it down in blood and bone.

91.

God flips through a magazine
while my teeth are drilled
haphazardly, like a bee buzzing against a window,

the dentist talking tennis with his assistant,
glancing at her cleavage over his mask,
as my eyes fill with tears,

until the end, when God rises from his chair,
smiling with pursed lips,
and opens his arms to me,

but I am too shy to go.

92.

I go to God with my cleverest ideas
but lose consciousness half way through my spiel,
bang my head on his desk

and avoid him on the street for the next week,
crossing to the other side when I see him coming
and ducking into the hardware store to hide

in the paint aisle,
which gives me an idea,
a new shade of sky blue,

and I go to my desk to design a lake to frame it.

93.

God feeds my fish while I am away,
pets the cat,
loses himself in the lava lamp,

the best of all possible deities,
friendly to my ficus tree, gentle with the ferns,
solemn with the mail,

and the worst of all the gods
because he is alone
and pages through my notebooks, opens drawers,

exposes himself at the window.

94.

I excuse myself from the table
to walk around the block wishing I hadn't eaten
or tasted the conversation,

preferring silence to flesh,
the company of wind skating over rooftops
to a dinner party of learned friends,

corpse-flies humming with full mouths
who dread not the solitude of the grave in the end
but the loneliness of the street after dark,

where I stand, nose in the air, sensing cautious joy.

95.

God prepares a special death for me,
a surprise party
which no one will attend,

unless I plan it myself,
comb my hair,
smile my gray smile,

touch the hand of each old friend
I still don't speak to
and look them in the eye,

cough a little, but hang on for a while.

95

96.

I live only for God,
for the possibility of perceiving
the meaning of a sparrow in mad flight,

or a river flowing,
a gust of wind playing across its surface
like heavy breathing,

or a train backing into the rail yard,
no mystery there,
but an impenetrable beauty

when the horn sounds in three short bursts.

97.

God acts a little crazy in my dreams,
giving back my presents,
cutting my face out of all our pictures,

not the one leaving,
and not as though he'll miss me when I'm gone
or grieve the loss of one creature,

yet passionate and nervous,
like he knows the plane is going down
and wants to say he loves me, loves everyone,

but clings ferociously to his insane secrecy.

98.

I walk away from my job at the uptown bistro,
bus the last tables, wash the dishes,
drag a barrel of garbage out to the alley,

and have a smoke,
smoke rising to a rectangle of sky,
no stars,

time to quit smoking, quit drinking, walk away
from the old, fat flies
whose simple hopes and complex palate cannot be satisfied

by any work of mine.

99.

God torments my free moments
which are many
with endless streams of words

rushing down endless mountains
too cold to drink
and in the middle of the sentence I run

one word
uttered once and tumbled down the streambed
over rocks

to some valley of death below.

100.

I brush my teeth correctly
rinse my face with water
but linger at the mirror

undress and fold my clothes
hang my belt on a hook
but linger at the window

but linger on my knees
fastidious in my prayers
turn down the bed sheets

but linger

101.

God passes through the garden in the winter
like a deer
leaving deep tracks in the stubble and snow,

wanders like Basho's dreams in withered fields,
an old man's dreams
nibbling the memory of food, nibbling weeds,

evergreen needles at the edge of the woods,
and saplings,
buds, bark, sustenance if sustenance is enough

for his ghostly genius, barely discernible in the mist.

RICHARD CARR grew up in Blue Earth, Minnesota, and now lives in Minneapolis. His honors include the Washington Prize for *Ace*, the Gival Press Poetry Award for *Honey*, and the Vassar Miller Prize for *Mister Martini*. He has had an assortment of odd jobs in restaurants, big box and small town hardware stores, book and newspaper print shops, and on farms, as well as house painting, cabinet making, ice rink grooming, and one summer filling sunken graves in a cemetery. As a teenager, he wanted to be a concert pianist. His cat's name is "Fur" Elise, and his goldfish are called Aria and Goldberg. In college, he majored in philosophy. At one time, he could recite a hundred digits of pi. He once hitchhiked to California. His car is a Jaguar XJ8. He's been in three motorcycle crashes. None fatal.

www.ingramcontent.com/pod-product-compliance
Lightning Source LLC
Chambersburg PA
CBHW061833040426
42447CB00012B/2943